Water Over Rock

Ron Thomas

Water Over Rock

Water Over Rock
ISBN 978 1 76109 324 1
Copyright © text Ron Thomas 2022

First published 2022 by
Ginninderra Press
PO Box 3461 Port Adelaide 5015
www.ginninderrapress.com.au

Contents

'10 Simple Things You Can Do Today That Will Make You Happier, Backed By Science' Bufferapp	9
Alone together	11
BLM?	12
Cobwebs	13
Does it seep into your latte?	14
Embryo	15
Forest Mist	16
How to break the mould?	17
In the Buffet at the Station – Epernay, France…	18
My Johari window's jammed	19
Lonely Fire – Miles Davis	20
Masterpieces	21
Nests	22
Out on a Limb	23
Sad last hours	24
At the Shady Lady Brothel – now BnB	26
Sweepings	28
On reading my 1981 Travel Diary	29
Warrandyte Thoughts	30
What matters is the build-up	31
At the Youth Hostel in my sixties	32
ANX	33
Branch Lines	35
Contact Us	36
Dog land	37
Emotional Archaeology	38
Framed	39
Pity Young Poets	40
Inverse Alzheimers	41

Last Hours in Sri Lanka	42
Lonely Planet	43
Meditation	44
Nightmares	46
Rhyll reflections	47
Sargasso	48
Us?	49
Fall of the Ronald Empire	50
Villanelle's villanelle	51
Water over rock	52
Word Play	53
Pigs fly	54
Apostrophe	55
Callistemon Drift	56
Crossing borders	58
Primary School Dress-up Day	60
English Teacher vs Society	61
Half Men Rap	62
I Rhyme Therefore I-amb	64
Jack of all Trades	65
Late	66
Long Haul Brain Carousel	67
Membrane	70
No adverbs, no adjectives	71
Satisfaction	72
Solitude	73
The One That Got Away	74
Blowing Leaves	75
What are you doing poem?	77
Writing My Aunt's Eulogy	78
Airport	79
Bas-relief	80

Camping Ground Off-season/Pa	81
Death Bed	83
Drought	84
Fading Vacation	85
Upon reading Hilary Mantel's Wolf Hall Trilogy	86
I would like	87
Jaffas Down the Aisle of Life	88
Leaf Blower	89
Mahabalipuram	90
Mother	91
Old T-shirt	92
Running Down	93
Shadow	94
Sovereign Citizen	95
These Words	96
Walking the dog	97
What do we do with all this death?	98
'You lookin' at me!'	99

'10 Simple Things You Can Do Today That Will Make You Happier, Backed By Science' Bufferapp

Momentum
    Muscles moving mass mesmerise

Shakespearean sleep
    That knits up the 'ravelled sleeve of care'

Philanthropy
    The virtue of vital volunteering

Smiling
    Hoist the flags of the lip corners

Gratitude
    Give thanks, be amazed at your luck, grin in disbelief

Cut the commute
    Diminish the disconnect, rescue time, inhabit home

Prepare plans
    Soar the imagination kite, plot the path – go if you must

Friends and family
    Frolic and fight, kin-connect, kith and make up

Al fresco
    Sun seek, oxygenate – get bird dappled and cloud licked

Meditate
    Magic mindfulness mitigates misery – permanently

If the above fails –
Grow old – it works!
Everything is behind you.

You are wise too!

Alone together

Conjoined
Pulsars self-orbiting
Sword against shield
Mace against helmet
    Needing the clang

Sick symbiosis
Your illness entraps me
Yet gives me purpose
Stifles but excuses
    All I can't be

Ear worm
I loathe your whine
My life's soundtrack
Fiendishly exacerbate it
    To fill the silence

Dependency
We are not liked
I'm sure it's you
Or what you have done to me
    Hate them together!

BLM?

Imagine if
your entrance caused
an emotional kaleidoscope
surprise, fear, paternalism, hostility

Imagine if
you were 'other'
in your own land
suspicious, enigmatic, inferior

Imagine if
after generations
of persecutions, discriminations, massacres
you were tokenised, appropriated, exploited

Imagine if
you'd lost
culture, language, country
then were told 'to snap out of it'

Imagine if
you were expected
to endorse a society
antithetical to your beliefs/poison to your kinship/ruinous to spirit

Imagine if
you were whiter
slender-nosed
a dominant history

Go on! Try it!

See how far you get.

Cobwebs

Glistening gossamer sky-traps impossibly strung across the moon
Dirty dangerous decrepitude in dusty attic disuse
Remnant memories, thought skeins, emotional detritus – the mind's lees
Dew dappled, diamond lacework in morning meadows

A lure to beautiful death
Blanketed in silk
Dissolved by injection
Innards sucked out
An empty carapace

Work of spin doctors

Does it seep into your latte?

Does it mar a fine cabernet?
Blackcurrant, raisin and   urine
Formaldehyded corpse
Stench of sleeping rough?

Can the first-class curtain stop
Battered wive's cries
Ice addicts' psychoses
Penetrating your world?

Can the high-fenced ivy-covered private school
Keep out the hungry
Ignorant bogans
Their violence and their tags?

> *Well my father employs a hundred*
> *And pays above award*
> *He fled Stalin's Iron Curtain*
> *Carrying only his shoes*
> *Worked 18 hour days*
> *Six days a week*
> *Enjoys a latte, a good red, education for his kids*
> *One he never had*
> *Now he funds a homeless shelter*

                                      Oh poet what do you?

Embryo

Tiny pebble
Love's ripple

Womb invader
Body possessor

Boy breaker
Dad maker

Family merger
Worlds crasher

Generation adder
'Grand' creator

Nameless faceless
DNA ladder

Your heart beat
A Taiko drum

Forest Mist

All analogies fail
At best hazy

Cold particulate air?
Dissolute soft floss?

Shaggy black/brown lances
Thrust skyward
Tipless
Leaf lost
Engulfed

Occasionally a grandfather tree
Tilted across the regiments
Broken limbed
Burl bunioned
Washed white slashes of bark
Collaged and twisted grey and brown

How to break the mould?

How to satisfy the unsatisfiable
    Mother
How to communicate with the incommunicable
    Father
Both dead?

How to unwind the DNA chains of
    familial bluntness
      work-drive'
        'Don't burn your bridges …'?

How to escape the magnifying glass burn
    of objectivity
      self-scrutiny
        comparability?

How to be freed
    from self-reliance
      introversion
        hunger for intensity?

And if I were…

        where would I be?

In the Buffet at the Station – Epernay, France, 8.30 a.m. Sunday

'Rock around the clock'
Scratches from the jukebox
The man with the too red face
Stands at the bar of his life
And sips a Sunday morning beer
With painstaking slowness

A train of Toute Grande Vitesse
Hums through the periphery of vision – and consciousness.

Les vendages, fingers red-as-grapes,
Drink their backaches as coffee
The tobacco in the young girl's 'rollie'
Is the eye of the vortex
Her whole being spirals about.
The black man sits – unsure, quiet.

The barmaid, still pretty, still laughing –
Not yet broken –
Feels the tug, awaits the pull,
Of the rough waters of the hard life
That will ultimately engulf her.
The work-bent men spar with her
In smiling complicity,
at their mutual fate.

My Johari window's jammed

Arena needs Windex
A strong rub with a scrunched up *Green Guide*
All of us need
Greater transparency

Rot in the lintels
Putty falling out
Paint peeling sill
Façade needs a facelift

Blind spot?
What blind spot?

Unknown
Who's looking in?
Who's looking out?
What's the view?

If I can't get this open
It's…
Curtains

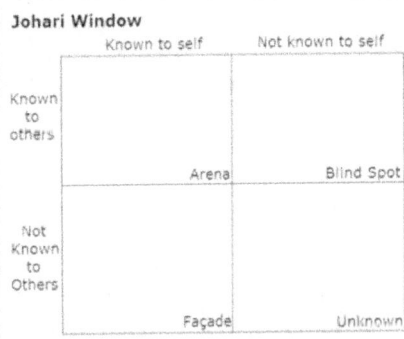

Lonely Fire – Miles Davis

Tiny bright trumpet flickers
Coolly dance above
Burbling piano

Solar flares of sax
Fly float and flop back
Sax cries – guitar echoes
Across a canyon of mud pool bass

Muted trumpet squeal flutters again
Far and plaintive
Pepper sprinkling percussion
Dots the landscape

Trumpet flare
Heaving piano/guitar magma
Bass bubble/sax sigh/percussion spice

Aural paella

Masterpieces

#1 – Diamond

Perfect planes exactly angled
Dazzling multifaceted mirrored triangles
    Gymnasium of light

#2 – Drawing

Picasso's pen
Four lines
Black on white
    quintessential buttocks

#3 *Of Mice and Men* – John Steinbeck

Lennie – disaster on a spider's web
George – finger in the dyke
Time, place – distilled, evoked
Characters – taut, clean – purpose perfect
Words – sifted, studied – only the best pearls
Narrative trajectory – unerring, unimaginable
– yet
Inevitable

If only life was
a diamond-etched narrative

Nests

Penguins pile pebbles
Fight beak to beak

Plovers
Plop eggs on sand
Raptor snacks
SUV carpets

Storks golliwog chimneys
Dreadlock skylines

Swallows clay mould
Or cobweb weave
Or build towers of spit
If only to make
Chinese soup

The busy sewing-machine beak is me
Pushing and prodding found objects
Into a crazy patchwork
Of life

Out on a Limb

An offshoot   of an offshoot   of an offshoot

A migrant leaf
of an Anglo-Celtic twig
of a Roman branch
of an Indo-European trunk
of a Homo Sapien tree
from a primate forest
– and summer is over

Sad last hours

Michelle

Two and a half hours in Mysore
Legendary palace ignored
Mouths trying
A 'Celebratory' puri
But it's not what they want

An intrusive American steals a couple of last minutes

Fingers know not what to do
Eyes swim

Two buses spew black smoke at each other

I, to Chenai
You, London

How far can a heart stretch?

Jane

You catch my eyes scudding to the window
See I'm not taking it well
In the spa your bikinied body glistens
Hours ago it was mine
I leap at you
       way too forcefully

Pam

'Make love one final time' she begs

So hurt
I'm pierced
    – relent

Once friendly skins try not to forget
Breasts sorrow against cold chest
Groin to groin

    Coming

      and

          going

At the Shady Lady Brothel – now BnB

Way out of town
In the jackrabbit scrub
Highway shy
In Nevada heat
Alone discrete
She waits

Park your rig
'Midst priapic peacocks
Penetrate– not iron filigree
But sagging olive-painted lattice
To fake Louis Fourteenth foyer
Wash the tumbleweeded road off
In a Mae West lipped bath

Chinoiserie room?
Cloissoné urns/tassled lamps
Black crimson and gold
Dragons rampant
Senorita in a cheongsam?

Aladdin's cave?
1001 Turkish delights
Rub the magic lantern
Release the seven veils
Of a 'trailer trash' Scheherazade

Cowboy cathouse?
Logs 'n' hide 'n' mounted deer
Rootin' tootin', cowboy bootin'
Calf-wrasslin'
A sad-eyed Minnehaha?

The mattress
is not
too good

Sweepings

Locks and tresses
Yesterday's look – Swept

Battered wives
Traumatised children – Swept

Mentally disabled
Job unable – Swept

Drunk, addicted,
Destitute – Swept

Peanut shells and human dreams
Feed the sewer rats

On reading my 1981 Travel Diary

Who is this boy?
This existential sponge
Boots tramping exotic tracks
Eyes agog

Synapses wildly firing
Impatient scrawlings
Knitting threads

Who are these ghosts of whom he speaks?
These Arak-crazed insights
Of five-minute friends
Dane, Austrian, French
Keenly seized in a Nepalese inn

Was it really me
Chillum high, Dada Dogged,* 'neath whirling lighthouse
beams on Trivandrum beach
Being pleasured by Michelle
Met just hours before?

Who is this youth?
His epiphanies?
Where?
When?

Ghost written
By
Myself

* German punk band

Warrandyte Thoughts

People create art – whilst ISIS beheads
Multiple ethnicities sip chais, eat polenta with fungi
On my tablet some imam says the world is still
A skateboarding youth laughs as he ollies over a sleeping dog
He carries no Kalashnikov
The watery winter sun wanly warms the fast denuding trees
The fire crackles merrily
Elsewhere stones crack bones –a careless girl has loved someone
She wasn't allowed to
The Yarra gurgles past the place museum photos show
The Wurrunjeri used to swim
Just outside our café window
Blood has gurgled too
The orange and almond cake is a delight

What matters is the build-up

What matters is the build-up
The rainless years before

The rest is just capricious
Highs and lows conjoining
Forcing furnace breath

Thunder bolt or careless camp
Exhaust spark or neglected wire

Which will deliver
Promised hell?

At the Youth Hostel in my sixties

The world's a bit dog-eared now
Smudged, torn
Begrimed and worn.
Or is that my dreams?
Chinese youths cook cabbage, rice and chicken
Inexpertly but with growing confidence – proudly
I once did noodles a la what-ever-I-could-find
In the gardens of Nice, moving the one burner stove
whenever the guard came by
We were cooking our lives – now gourmet is a breeze.
Yet a flavour is missing
Eau de Jeunnesse?
Naivety?

30 years ago I gave a Viking funeral to my travel boots
Scarred by Cretan rocks, dyed by Delhi dust and cracked by
Nepali snow
I've become them.
Now these Nordic girls
So tight skinned
Exploring my country
Map themselves.
I've been to more of theirs than they have,
Thrown pathways 'cross the globe
I'm no interest to them
Though we tramp the same globe
    Theirs is new
        And mine is not.

ANX

>Perturbations
>Grating of Celestial Spheres
>Inaudible seismic trembling
>Tumbling certitudes
>Silently cascading masonry

I

>>Running faster
>>On a faster decaying treadmill
>>Chimerical
>>Incorporeal
>>Tempested
>>A lame ant
>>Not even 'ragged claws'
>>Appearing, disappearing
>>Circling on mosaics

ET

>>French 'and' – more
>>Indian-lined ridge top
>>Legal mail by signature
>>Needed number on a flat phone
>>Password forgotten
>>WiFi-less
>>A perfectly benign sky – cracking

Y?

> No reply
> The indifferent universe
> Indifferent
> The unbelieved-in gods
> Unavailable
> For a quick conversion
> A trackless sand dune sea
> Identical in all directions

Branch Lines

Beneath Eurostar
off the Intercity tracks
lie branch lines
Far from the flashy flyovers
one man ferries
muscle cars across
Off the A, B and C roads
walls and hedges have primacy
and tarmac dips under streams
On mountain passes
there's no overtaking
brakes are life
On branch lines
the train driver stops for eggs

Contact Us

In the fine print
Bottom of the web site
If you fit the categories
There is a link
01
But first
Does your unique inquiry
Fit the FAQs?
(Or is that FUs?)
10
No?! Then email
First:
Your name, family tree, grandma's bra size, security code,
DNA and favourite Linux program
Nature of your request:
Select from drop-down menu
No drop-down menu!!
@#%&
If you are having trouble
Please contact
+44 5462 8124595 67989992
Just 10p per minute plus international connection fees plus tax
plus foreign currency conversion rates – credit card fees apply
Our office is open after 15.00 GMT for 30 seconds
'Your call has been placed in a queue'
Air Fair?
Not likely

Dog land

They speak bark
Any non-dog scented
And the chain of sentries
Sets off like beacon fires

Demented in their enclosures
They repeat their instinctual
Territorial imperatives
Until the threat passes
And another comes along
Ad nauseam

Stop the boats

Emotional Archaeology

Run the surveying transit
Across sulci and gyri
Map mind

Stake memories
String/grid/coordinate
Family/friends/frustrations

Pickaxe and shovel down
Wheelbarrow out
Thoughts/feelings/desires

Saw through rationalisations
Defence mechanisms/ego constructs
Hit hurt/fear/vulnerability

Mason trowel insecurities/shames/disgusts
Delicately lever darknesses into light
Nudge fantasies out of cracks

Brush away guilts/psychological imperatives
Dustpan self-loathings
Bucket prevarications

Shake-screen behaviours/feedback/self-knowledge
Collect artefacts of insight
Flecks of truth

Rebury quickly!

Framed

The innocent
Are hanged by it

We know it
From windows
And mirrors too

Pictures are nothing without it
Though some 'push the envelope'
Peep 'outside the square'

What is Art but framing?

Rambunctious life though
Splinters gilt wood
Cracks marble
Eludes words
And won't canter to iambic pentameter

This poem
the bolt click echo
of a now horseless
stable

Pity Young Poets

Trying to make sense of
the same firsts
as the Ancients:
flesh, love, the stars – identity
betrayal

The latest ripple
(after rollers past)
trying to scale
the beach –
to nibble at man's
sandcastles

New Sisyphi
hoping this time
the rock will hop
the centuries-old groove

Inverse Alzheimers

Peeling spuds
>*Camp kitchens Broome to Portland Oregon*
>*Curl off my knife*

Watching king parrots
>*Blue-footed boobies, frigate birds, wandering albatross*
>*Wing out from Galapagos/Antarctica*

'*Bonjour*' French vanners at Olinda Falls
>*Our van dying in Morocco, old Holdens wheezing to the Gulf*
>*Wheel into mind*

Pungent tomato
>*Garlicked Spanish peasant bread, Sri Lankan curry, Peruvian ceviche*
>*Tantalise my mouth*

Persecuted Palestinians, generous Greek peasants, Dutch novelists
>Cascade

Mdina castle, Kanazawa tea shop, Patagonian parilla
>Tempt

Annapurna, Amazon, Yellowstone, Narvik
>Blur

Too much world
For one head

Last Hours in Sri Lanka

Overlapping frames

    Old city walk – stench, deprivation and alleyway cricket
    Luxury boutique hotel – massage, meditation and design
    Buddhist Poya holiday – full moon shining on mystic milky stupas
    Our last supper – French Burgundy and gastronomic curries

Super-impositions

    Statues of the Virgin in Hindu hues
    swim amid Muslim headscarves Sari bright
    Buddhist chants entwined in muezzin wails
    waft round KFC and designer chic
    Guide, Namunu, taking his tip and smiling farewell
    – thinks of his next clients
    Colombo airport
    – hours of modern tedium fade into Singapore

Jump cut

Lonely Planet

Guidebooks imply it needs companions
But it is swarming with them

Like a dog with mange it can't reach its pain
Armless it can't scratch
Mouthless it can't shriek

It needs a nurse
With a lot of Savlon

Meditation

    Comfort on
    Eyes off
    Hands cupped
    In Out
    In Out
     'Breakfast?'
    No
    Thought dismissed
     'I forgot…'
    No
    Relax
     'I really should…'
    S T O P I T
    Smile
    Be calm
    Becalm
    In n n n
    Out t t t

                          Brain silence

emergent fuzzy textures   greyish gun-blue swirls
grids, waves, giant weaves
kaleidoscoping

clouds part   aerial views   beach crescents
jungle hung rock humps
soundlessly screening
incorporeal

falling back
back into –   dream drift   sky float
mesmeric miasma

time's
milestones
melt

stockinged stillness steals in
holding hands with quietude

In   Out
Out

Nightmares

> Like farcical sausages
> Dream men meander
> Past sombre houses
> Where dead dogs accuse

Razor blades rain slicing cheeks and eyeballs
Heroes' zombie carcasses are trundled off
To museums of rotted ambitions
stillborn dreams/bottled foetal hopes

> Motorbike doesn't start/push it
> station road steepens/asphalt turns glue
> Platforms deform/ticket offices flee
> Trains infinitely delay/switch lines
> express-by horns jeering

Children play in addict filled parks
Paedophiles rain sweets
flashers scuttle like crows
Emaciated tattooed teens
drug addled sell their filthy bodies
Pimps finger guns and each other

> Family estate overrun by partisans
> What war? What side? What end?
> Smash doors to seize your children
> Arm them to kill you

Ancestral soils patiently diligently nurtured planted watered protected
succumb to dust

> Good – evil's slave
> Beauty – decay's toy

Rhyll reflections

limpid
      still

          dew-lift quiet
                mist-fall soft

dream drift ripples
      pebble tickle

          silken sea
                unmoving mirror

white sails slump
      water colour wash

                        lucent pier to nowhere

          tran..

          quil..

          it..

          y

Sargasso

Every crossroad has four triangles where no tyres tread
    Bits of accidents
        Truck spills
            Butts and squashed cans
            Congregate
    Enough dirt to grow weeds

Every ocean has an eddy like a bathplug hole drawing
    Wood and nets
        Polystyrene and plastic
            Even shipping containers
                Rubbish-based life evolves

Every society has its ever-growing Charybdis sucking
    The homeless and antisocial
        The addicted and insane
           The dangerous and criminal
                Into a desperate spiral of venom

In the corners of every mind detritus of
    Tweets and ads
        Fake news/puerility
            Celebrity puff/pompous hype
            Congeal

        Enough dirt to grow weeds

Us?

She

J
o
n
q
u
i
l
i
a
n

I

Red Hot Poker

Bobbing

        about

Fall of the Ronald Empire

Arthritis in the colonies
Vandalised aqueducts

Huns pain my shoulders
Immune-slaves revolt

Visigoths assault the eardrums
Slow decay the eyes

Rebel hairs break away
Borders sag and crack

Body's legions – battle scarred and stiff
Caesars of memory – in disarray

Et tu, Brute?

Villanelle's* villanelle

Villanelle loves to kill
Do we believe it is Eve?
Can she maintain the eve-il?

Will they partner for ill?
Or is Eve just naïve?
Villanelle loves to kill

She has shown Eve the thrill
Does she really believe
She can maintain the eve-il?

Or a love so feral
Both cannot bear to leave?
Villanelle loves to kill

Hunted and huntress still
Eve stabs, Vill shoots, both grieve
Can they maintain the eve-il?

Love and death and chill skill
A tapestry they weave
Villanelle loves to kill
Can she maintain the eve-il?

* *Killing Eve,* TV femme psychopath villanelle

Water over rock

Dimpling shifting sheens
Silken shimmers
Caressing smoothing brightening

Burbling cadences flow
Ever the same/never the same
Like passing Stone Age grunts/Ancient Greek/modern English
Conceptualising knowing understanding

Infinitesimally atom by atom
Liquid grinds solid
Sluicing shaping sculpting
Like Ra/Zeus/Allah/Einstein
Tinkling the brain's wrinkles and crinkles
Civilising socialising educating

Bright metaphors cascade
Images coruscate
Alliteration and assonance bounce and splash
Hard/soft against the granite of dross
Shining it mirror-like
Turning up the technicolour
Enlivening enhancing enchanting

Log falls
Stream diverts
Lights out

Word Play

S
    L
     I
          D
GREW
B   u   c   d
   o   n   e

T   h r   e   w

Oops
    d
    r
    o
    p
    p
    e
    d
one
bro
k e n

Pun   nuP   Palinindrome

OonerSpism

Le' go

Pigs fly

A train disrupting earthquake reveals a pre-dawn Kanpur, a dream's death, a man's lost night. Long-haired pigs snout the blackness munching litter and depriving the sacredly starving bag-o'-bones cows. Pre-empting the first Tuk Tuk's cancerous cough, nuzzling dieselised dust, seeking – and gobbling – human faeces, they briefly dominate earth.
Shoddy corruptly understrength concrete hole-in-the-wall shops, still grilled, decay silently under tropical rot. Luridly painted, a trishaw lottery cart, wheels wobbling arthritically, threadbare tyred, squeaks of tickets to salvation. Shiva, reincarnated as beggar, lifts his newspaper bed, puts his hand out to the blind universe yet again.
A turbaned man in shalwar kameez older than time and dictator dirty, throws up a hooked wire into a spaghetti of lines sparking the dark and setting alive trishaw lights and screeching Indian pop, a knife slash across a weary centuries-old dawn reluctantly fingering tufts of hair on a pig tiptoeing for a putrid banana skin wedged in a crack – and urinating his hopes for the day.

Apostrophe

The mark that most of us will leave
Is, at best,
An apostrophe

Callistemon Drift

A vermillion tide fringes the pavement
    Not blood
    Not terrorism
A feathering of bottlebrush spines

A seduction of advertising
    Not flowers
    Not art
Jangles the walls

An anger of graffiti
    Not kind words
    Not hugs
Snarls from concrete

Coughs of diesels
    Not perfume
    Not azure blue
Belch from truck holes

A vroom-swish of cars
    Not music
    Not laughter
Sound tracks us

A hate-din of media
        Not encouragement
        Not celebration
Corrodes our harmony

But we'll fix it
With bollards and CCTV
More durable
Than callistemon

Crossing borders

Two solo backpackers
In love with the world
Met in Hamburg
City of sailors and sex

Brazilian Paulo
Latin tactility
Castro beard
Guevara charisma

Down the Reeper Bahn
Bar/Sex shop/Casino/Bar
Hookers every two metres
We poured out our travels

A beautiful girl
In jumper and jeans
Took my arm
'Willst du mit mir schlafen?'

'Let's go to Belgium'
Said Paulo
We could
We did

Sick of partying Italians
In sleepless dorms
I snuck us into
A closed one

I awoke penis between legs
Not mine
Hand around penis
Not mine

'Sorry I'm not gay,' I said

Hasty retreat
Embarrassed breakfast
Different borders

Primary School Dress-up Day

Peppa Pig gets the tap out
But Dorothy the Dinosaur's too slow
Sponge Bob handpasses to Spider Man
Spider Man to Whimpy Kid who fumbles
Crumbed by Henry the Octopus
Short Kick to Captain Underpants
Eludes Wonky Donkey
Brushes aside Captain Feathersword
Bluey brings him down
Hermione blows the whistle
It's a free to Cuddlepie
Who runs past Snugglepot
Sells the dummy to Harry Potter
And puts it through
As the playtime siren sounds
It's Fairy Magic 3 wands 2 spells
Triumphant over Naughty Elves 2 wands 1 spell

Now it's maths

English Teacher vs Society

Students need to develop a built-in 'crap detector'

Think clear
        Obfuscate
Message
        Messenger
Nuance
        Generalise
Empathise
        Stereotype
Sensitivity
        Troll
Literacy
        Tweet
Subtlety
        Sloganise
Explore
        Block
Truth
        Alternative facts
Depth
        Simplicity

        Trumped

Half Men Rap

Sincere smiles with crossed fingers
Core and non-core
Rotten to the core
Half men
Loyalty above right
Party above all else
Half men
Machiavellian micro-men
Half-rate invertebrates
Half men
Discount values
'Down, down, our integrity's down'
Half Men
Pinocchios of pressure groups
Thunderbirds on lobbyists' strings
Half Men
Purveyors of popularism
Imprisoned in privileges

Half Men

Semi truths are steamed in sins of omission, garnished with
selectivity, short term thinking sprinkled, self-serving fear
Tabascoed, served with mirrors and smoke – an indigestible joke

Half Men

Captive to the shock-jock sloganisers, hate mongers,
demonisers, dealers in doggerel and slaves to stereotypes;
their painted Luna Park mouths mouth emptiness in a rigor
mortis 'public face' whilst they swear and knive, connive and
lie whilst a planet dies – and their buddies thrive

Half Men

Half suit

I Rhyme Therefore I-amb

Like a mumbling muslim
Who On –a -mat –a- ppears
I'm in terror of dactyls
And find Ana a pest
I've tried synaesthesia
To the point of amnesia
Took my chance with assonance
Tried to dance with dissonance
Alliterated until sated
Then silly me
Tried simile.

Got metaphorical
Whilst being allegorical
Was no poorer
For using anaphora
Not that I antithesise
Prefer to hyperbolise

I'm under no illusion
I'm without a good allusion
And being an amateur
At writing pentameter
I think it quite archaic
Trying to be trochaic!

And if A is phorism
Then what is B for?

Jack of all Trades

If I had dedicated myself to one thing

This poem would've been longer

And better

Late

    night

        pi

            an

                o

Melancholy staircase
    Late night piano
        Stiletto on cobbles
            Late night piano
                Drunken keys
                    Late night piano
                        Tinkling frayed dreams
                          Late
                                night
                                      piano
                              Pulp fiction trills
                        Late night piano
                  Ashtray of hope
              Late night piano
            Desultory rain
        Late night piano
      Arpeggio of pain
Late night piano
    Alone
        Again
Late
    night
        pi
            an
                Oh!

Long Haul Brain Carousel

Pre-dawn gaucho/tango/Peronista taxi
Bag-drop snake
Metal detected/inspected/seat selected
    Thump

Plane-poured next country
Empanadaed/caffeinated/device fuelled
Queued/swiped/greeted/seated
    Bump

'The Bride Stripped Bare'
'Fell asleep inside you –
Shows how much I love you'
Non-orgasmic reading
    Flop

Search Entertainment – appropriately 'Babel'
Traumatised/Naked/Deaf-mute/Japanese girl
Sister-perving/Tourist-killing/Moroccan boy
Wedding-attending/Children-losing/Mexican nanny
Dali Air?
    Clunk

White noise roar
365 time-slaying zombie screens
Babies akimbo
Heads knee-dangling
Headphone vice/Armrest assault/Buttock revolt
  Screech

'Hurt Locker' – Boy-body death trap
'Fish or chicken?'
Padlocked suicide-bomb victim
'Red or white wine?'
  Bang!

Cartoon plane
Night shadow chased
Porthole-laser slices/closes
False night re-falls
  Crash

Fake dawn/fake food/limp time
'Mythos'
Phaeton losing the horses
15,000 km
Clipping his heals
  Clop

Next country – ours
Transit purgatory – near yet far
Final flight/disembark/check/claim/customs
Goggle-eyed familiarity
The 'Tulla', our road
    Drop

Membrane

Translucent meniscus
Tautly curved – reflective yet transparent
Impossibly slight

Delicate as thistle down
But as dividing as a jet window
We're separated by shine

Fingers stretch it
Lips press at it
Still the barrier

Fists punch it
Reflections distort –
Like disturbed water –
Rebound and settle

Bubble balloons
Only atoms thick
Our minds try to pierce it

Walk away

No adverbs, no adjectives

I eat
Walk
Lie
Dream

I cycle
Strain oxygenates
Wellness invades
Happiness comes
Sentences truncate

I read
Worlds open
Characters bloom
Mind resets

I write
Painting without colours
Nuance deprived

Like a world without art

Satisfaction

Is
A fire's warmth
From logs tree-felled sawn/split/barrowed and stacked by my hand

Is
A globe circled
Planned and implemented/improvised and chanced/safe and solo

Is
A woman's love
Forgiven faults/given body/food offerings/friendship

Is
Two children
Independent/loving/compassionate/moral and free

Is
A devoted dog
Licks and nudges/lap sitter/proud carrier of sticks

Is
Meaningful work
Fabulous feedback/inspiring others/validation

Is
Wrangling words
Into an almost-perfect shape

Solitude

Din dwindles disperses dies
Tension unknots frays fades
Sun warms roof creaks
Dog sighs
Fire fitfully flickers
Pie eaten coffee sipped apple crunched
Only me

Random images – Mekong island Salinas restaurant – swim
Tickling the lobes
As the fire toes

Poems sprout
Stillness

Way above a jet rumbles
350 people, flying can

King parrots bicker over grain

I
    peck
           at
                  mind
                        seeds

The One That Got Away

It scintillated
silken silver
alliterative assonant onomatopoeic

Metaphors extended
it eagled
forensic-eyed

Fox-sly
it murdered its chickens
deft swift
surprising yet perfect

Allusions twinkled
apt esoteric – dense
Tygers burning bright

Lacerating visceral humanity
entwining balletic-light profundity
blood rivers delta-ing hope

Neural nibbles
rhythmic tugs
bobbing float

But hooked
only this tiddler

Blowing Leaves

Flurrying flock
    Twisting turning
      Yellow-fish school
        Of May morning memories

Hugging Clydesdale legs
    Car-doored thumb
        Multi-storeyed treehouse
Mum-pus and Gyp
    'Gentlemanly behaviour an example to the class'
      A mother's proud beam
Solitary hayshed vistas
    Biking the Murray floodplain
        Tess's taut breasts
Alma Road Boarding house
    Melbourne High coldness
        Alone in the world

Yellow-white-yellow
    Chasing each other
Rex/Rob/Ron
    T.S. Eliot/Bertolucci/Dali
        Uni/politics - the draft
Class – only five years younger
    New car/girlfriend/Noosa
        Hiking/4WDriving/booze
Finding world/losing father
    Climbing ladder
        Donning mortgage

Hangi home wedding
    Birthing three

               Losing one

Warping wave
    Escher birds
Parental pyrotechnics
    Bunger shocks
      Explosive ecstasies
        Damp squibs
          Finally rockets

Mum – slipping away

Distillation/relaunch/refresh
    Refind the world
      Another career
          Welcomed across the nation

Our daughter's a bride

There's

      still

            wind

What are you doing poem?

What are you doing poem
Pulling me out of bed?
Who gave you permission
To infiltrate my head?

You sit me on the toilet
In cardigan and slippers
Phone but no glasses
Dictating in the dark

Writing My Aunt's Eulogy

91 years
Few witnesses
Alive

Phonebook
Friends now crosses
Replacements
Doctors
Last known addresses
Pre-nursing home
Pre-grave

Her children
Anonymously fathered
Adopted out
Unacknowledged
Unable to be acknowledged
Un
Both coming to…
Hope the corpse will say
What the woman couldn't
For 75 years?

How am I
To find truth
For this
Unverifiable
Fiction?

Airport

3 a.m. blear
Flakes of consciousness
I am a passport
Limp kids
Automaton mums
Umbilicalled to sleep
Morn murks
Shops yawn
First espresso sputters
Grim rays flare
'Have you got…?'
Gate change
Motherboards warm
Lists load
Listless
Hi-vis bees swarm
Winged queen
Pumping kerosene
Queues caterpillar
Packs drag
'What's the delay?'

    Attenuation

                    Attenuating

Bas-relief

Our parents chisel madly
From mirror images
At unformed rock – or not

School friends gouge and cut
Teachers rub little bits
To a nice polish

At uni besotted by other poses and poseurs
We brandish our own hammers
To the pre-cuts
Craft elaborate curlicues of pretension
A Romantic ear
A Gothic stare

Our lovers try to tidy up the mess
Into their likeness

In old age we abandon work
Admire what's complete
Acknowledge the huge cliff face
From which we partly peep

Camping Ground Off-season/Pa

Jumping pillows lie limp
ghost thumps and squeals
still echo
Pa nods
Power poles have lost their umbilicals
yellow patches
a vanishing silver-tarp settlement
of generations barbecuing memories
Pa dribbles
Stubbies full of stories
wet year, scorcher
baby chasing kangaroo
toddling, then training wheels
on the Xmas bike
Pa snorts
Catching dad at beach cricket
kissing the cousin
not even liked
hanging in the dunes with new kids
blackberry nip erasing inhibitions
dissolving bikini straps
Pa grins
Caught drunk by 'disappointed' parents
didn't go the next year
then girlfriend one – awkward
others
then the one
Pa sighs

Pegs pulled
last trip to amenities
ocean beating time
ocean beating time
ocean beating time
Time

Death Bed

On my death bed
I'd like to say 'sorry'

To the 'others':
In my 30s and 40s
Who endured my unbridled hubris
                      Mortality a distant thing

To F:
Who I strung along,
Out of loneliness and lust,
Long after my passion had fled

To R:
So young and troubled,
Who I slept with anyway –
Bodies being simpler
Than unique minds

To C:
Whose love
Mine never matched
        And she never knew

But on our death beds
It's too late to say – 'sorry'.

Drought

There's coolness in the gullies
Sun's razor hasn't hit
A red-hot poker sky
Hasn't cauterised it yet

Flies mill on corpses
Skulls poke through wool
Dam-denied, red-dusted
Cows' tongues atrophy

Furnace ups a notch
Eucalypts jettison shade

Then stillness, baking stillness
Desiccates the bones

Fading Vacation

Leaves are yellowing
Time takes shape
      insistently so

Gadgets are leaking home
Mundanity wets our feet

We're almost sated with Ozymandiases,
Fallen empires and kings

      And then

In Galleria Villa Borghese
Across the centuries
Marble-fleshed
Daphne
Is becoming
A laurel tree

Upon reading Hilary Mantel's *Wolf Hall* Trilogy

'How do I love thee?'*
Winnowing a million haystacks
For a pincushion of dazzling needles
Inhabiting a Cromwell, a king, a time
Marshalling a constellation of characters
Voicing basest male
And subtlest poet
Trawling the literary aphorisms
For the exact catch
Holding back a modern sensibility
No feminist disdain
No parable chains
Reader 'it once was thus'
Make of it what you will

And where do we start?
A character incessantly puppeteering
His Damoclean sword – the King
Jousting and bear baiting
The 'greenscreen' fill
Behind people like us
Caught in an older vice
Machiavellian pan-European politics

Mirror and Light

I throw this pathetic cloak
At your bejewelled feet

* Elizabeth Browning

I would like

I would like to believe
    News isn't fake
        The state benign
            Tyrants must fail
                Electors can't be bought
                    Democracy works

I would like to believe
    Wealth doesn't trump law
        Criminals are caught
           Firms aren't corrupt
                Our future is nor Dark Webbed

I would like to believe
    Automation controllable
        Genetic engineering safe
           Science has answers

I would like to believe
    My children's lives will not be worse
        My grandchildren will inhabit a kind planet

I would…

    I did…

            Once

Jaffas Down the Aisle of Life

Little brother
Bad day
Cuddles dog
'Gyp knows that I are poor'

> Farm child
> Every morning
> Father chills me
> 'On we go with can we take it'

> Kotta Xmas
> Nan asks pop
> If he liked the meal
> 'Didn't hear me complain did ya?'

Boarding house boy
Room-mate shower-sings
His pre-horse race mantra
'A shit, a shave, a shower and shampoo'

Backpacking India
Alone and ill
Chance encounter
'Come share my room'

Hairs
      on a
                      sticky lolly

Leaf Blower

All day he blew leaves
Trying to tidy up
Trying to be – one of us

But he didn't look like 'us'
And leaf blowers – being annoying
The lads – they bashed him up

In Sudan he'd seen a little girl
Macheted at his feet

Now he lies with her

Leaves upon a street

Mahabalipuram

Tamil Nadu, India

A decaying near-half-century Kodak slide reveals
Seven granite-hewn chariot temples driving into sea
Arjuna's seven austerities
Conjure the Descent of the Ganges from heaven
Shiva's hair protecting earth from its impact
Or was it to gain Shiva's sword? Or both?
One and a half millennia obscure the path

Arriving by diesel chariots
An Australian (sick and liquid) and an Austrian
United in awe
Sit sun-warmed astride
A mammoth granite Ramayana
Midst Brahma bulls and Ganesh elephants
Carved before countries

Three coast clawing tsunamis
A half bull ocean rise
Now drown lions and horses
That slaves, workers and worshippers
Chiselled for centuries
Shiva's hair insufficient
To prevent Neptune claiming it all

Mother

Warm still
Still warm
Still

An hour ago
You breathed
Your mouth is open
Unable to catch
        The air

The sun is rising
But you are not
You are not
Not   you are

Old T-shirt

Bought in days of wonder
Elephant sunset
Sticky rice Beer Lao
'Good Evening Luang Prabang'

Drenched in squash sweat
Wine splashed
Tear rained
Ripped off for love

Washed tumbled
Hung
Sun faded

Snagged patched
Seams parting
Threads hanging

Not stretched 'cross sick bloated belly
Nor drooped 'cross withered still chest
Still wearable

Now work shirt
Paint speckled
Grass seeded
Oil and bloodstained

Logo just legible

Comfy

Running Down

Growing up, falling down
Food and drink
Gulp them down
'Blowing up' – run it down

Sister frowns
'Not you too, Mel!'
Sister – kin of bone
Ran it down, ran it down

Mother cries
Keeps things clean
Chases dust
Runs it down, runs it down

Pretty Mel
Wears down the flesh
With
      fatal
        steps
Running down

Shadow

I have a white shadow
It's always underfoot
It follows at night
The sun doesn't blacken it
Other shadows only dim it
It's nothing like me
I have two legs
Hamish has four

Sovereign Citizen

So you are

> Sovcit
>   Sovereign citizen
> Incel
>   Involuntarily celibate

Well I'm

> Inpo
>   Involuntarily poor
> Inano
>   Involuntarily anonymous
> Insi
>   Involuntarily sick
> Inde
>   Involuntarily detained
> Nosov
>   No sovereignty

Why don't you try

> Volsa
>   Voluntary saint
> Or
> Volkin
>   Voluntarily kind

These Words

These Words want to hurt you
They want to tear at the fine-tune of your eyes
Oh yes
And These Words want to rape you
Just so
You never
Regard

These Words

The same way
Again

Walking the dog

Leaves in autumnal pall
Caged cocky mimicking dogs
Day-abandoned houses
The odd toddler toddling
Paedophile's picking
'I've seen too many cop shows'

Empty driveways like mute tongues
What are they asking?

I'm doing my circuit in reverse
To be different
Is it different?
Poetic impulses come upon me

Why must I try to wring meaning
From distant dog barks, whispering gums and potholes?

What do we do with all this death?

After visiting the corpses in Palermo Catacombs

Dress it in its Sunday best
Cellar it
– like wine?
How many centuries?
Embalm it
So the memory lives on
Long after the rememberers are gone?

Perpetually two years old
   to my grandmother
      mother
         me
            my daughter
              and hers
                  If we had all passed this way?

But we haven't passed THIS way
Some are buried
Some ash
Some may be frozen – revived?
Some may not die
Embalmed alive
on skyscrapers
of bones.

'You lookin' at me!'

'inner disarmament…is what humanity needs.' – Dalai Lama

Our brains are a Somme of trenches
Synapses sniping
Lobes lobbing
Bayonet plunges of sarcasm
Razor wit lining parapets of prejudice
Our best ideals boat people
Our empathy in detention

Our mind –
That chip on our shoulder.

www.ingramcontent.com/pod-product-compliance
Lightning Source LLC
Chambersburg PA
CBHW071126130526
44590CB00056B/2510